Investing Basics

presents:

Successful Forex Trading For Beginners

Making Money with Forex Trading within a Few Moments!

F.R. Commerce

Special thanks to:

The Investing Basics Team

The Foreign Exchange Investors Association

Forex Trading Group

Forex Investing Club

Business and Investors Association

and many more people who have helped contribute to this work

Introduction

You know how that saying goes, "Money makes the world go round".

Nowadays, for you or anyone to live comfortably, you should have enough money to buy the things you need. Food, shelter, water, a way to get around, everything.

However, a lot of people are currently experiencing that grueling feeling of living from paycheck to paycheck and they are barely surviving the day. Since their job would probably take most of their hours in a day, there is not much time for them to take on another job. And trust me, a lot of colleague, friends, and myself have been there. It sucks. Period.

There are several options that you can take in order to solve this problem: one is to scrimp on the daily necessities and save up (and invest in time deposits, mutual funds or stocks), and another is to find other ways to make money without hurting your day job. The first one is definitely painful; to do away with enjoying life and its luxuries just to save a meager amount isn't fair. What's the point of saving up if you don't make enough money in the first place? That leaves everyone to resort to the other, better option.

Through foreign exchange trading, you can definitely make money in the comfort of your home and at your own pace. With the advent of technology, trading through the foreign exchange, or Forex for short, has become a lot easier; everyone can trade with other people from anywhere in the world.

Forex is definitely advantageous compared to other investment vehicles. In Forex, you trade yours or people's money through an online platform to gain a profit. And there is no person in the world that doesn't need money, so there will always be somebody who is willing to buy Forex. It's very easy to sell; that's why the profits are instantaneous – no more waiting time needed unlike in other investments such as time deposits and mutual funds.

More importantly, there is an unlimited earning potential in Forex. In other financial instruments, such as savings deposit and fixed income securities, the income is already defined by the fund manager. In Forex, it is you, the trader, who has the control of the earnings.

This book will teach you how to start trading successfully in Forex and make your money work for you - literally.

PART I: What Forex Trading is and How it Works

Chapter 1: What is Forex and How Does It Work?

Foreign exchange is the biggest financial market in the world - with a global market value of $5 trillion.

Forex is simply the process of exchanging a currency with another currency on its current exchange rate.

The exchange is done primarily because of commerce and tourism. For example, let's say a person is travelling to Japan. He will exchange his US dollars for Japanese yen so he could pay for the things he needs when in Japan.

In the business sector, products and services may come from a different country. Let's say, a US car company may import parts from Japan and thus have to pay the products in Japanese yen. So again, the exchange is required, which is usually done by the companies' banks.

Because of the massive exchange of currencies every day, among many factors, it creates a difference in the value of the currencies being traded. This price difference creates a financial opportunity, which is now called Forex market trading.

What is Forex Market Trading?

Banks who were originally trading currencies for their clients saw this opportunity and began trading their money - in the hopes that the currency they bought will increase in value. They also hope that the currency they sold will be weaker in the near in the near future.

Although the difference is small, if trading in enormous amounts, this small price difference in buying and selling currencies can still rake in millions in profits within a single day. Yes, it's possible, though it's usually a larger-scale operation.

This opportunity to trade currencies was then sought out and grabbed by large corporations, multinational companies, a few wealthy private individuals, and hedge funds.

Basically, Forex market trading is the process of buying and selling currencies with the goal of making profit from the price difference. It's just buy-low, sell-high, only with currency.

Major Currencies

Anyone in the world can participate in the Forex market and trade their own currency against any other currency.

However, just like any industry, there will always be major participants.

Below is a short list of major currencies being traded and their corresponding symbols:

Country	Currency	Symbol
United States	US dollar	USD
Euro Zone Members	Euro	EUR

Japan	Japanese yen	JPY
Great Britain	Pound	GBP
Switzerland	Swiss franc	CHF
Canada	Canadian dollar	CAD
Australia	Australian dollar	AUD
New Zealand	New Zealand dollar	NZD

It is important to become familiar with the currency symbols as these symbols are used when trading.

The first two letters of the currency symbol is from the country's name and the last letter is from its currency's name. For Switzerland, the symbol is CHF as Switzerland's official name, which is in Latin, is Confoederatio Helvetica.

Major Currency Pairs

When you take part in the Forex market trading, you are trading in pairs or currencies. Essentially, you are simultaneously buying and selling currencies.

For example, if you buy Japanese yen with US dollars, you are simultaneously selling your US dollars. Below is the list of major currency pairs being traded:

- EUR/USD

- USD/JPY

- GBP/USD

- USD/CHF

- AUD/USD

- NZD/USD

If you noticed, in every pair, the US dollar is in one side.

Nearly 85 percent of all Forex transactions have the US dollar in one side, making it the most traded currency.

This is because, aside from the United States being the largest economy in the world, the US dollar is also the reserve currency, which means it is often used in international transactions. In the Forex world, when people just say "dollar," they are usually referring to the US dollar.

When trading without the US dollar, even if the currencies being traded are major currencies, like EUR/CHF, they are being referred to as minor currency pairs.

What Makes the Forex Market Different?

Unlike the New York Stock Exchange or other financial markets, which have some physical, central location for all their transactions, Forex is tagged as over-the-counter. Why? Because everything is done electronically within a huge networks of banks around the globe, 24 hours a day and five days a week.

So, wherever your location is, you can easily participate in the market.

Additionally, traders can also choose who they want to make a transaction or trade with. But that also depends on the conditions offered by the counterpart trader, their reputation, and price.

Although financial, commercial, and tourism transactions play a huge part in the Forex market, speculators play a bigger chunk of it. These are individuals and companies who buy and sell currencies based on their price movement.

In fact, around 90 percent of the volume being traded daily is from these institutions. This massive Forex transaction in almost any given time makes the market very liquid. Liquidity is an important factor in any financial market, as it allows buying and selling currencies in huge volumes without causing significant movement in prices or exchange rates.

Although the words FOREX trading may sound complicated, it basically is the same as what is called "direct access trading" of various types of foreign currencies. Until recently, FOREX trading could only be practiced by large and imminent banks and traders. However, due to recent advancements in technology have provided small banks and traders with the opportunity to utilize FOREX trading. They mostly practice it through online platforms.

FOREX trading always takes place in pairs such as USD/ Pound, Pound/Yen or Euro/USD. The exchange rates between any two currencies changes on a regular basis. According to a study, around 85 percent of daily exchanges involve trading between any two major currencies of the world.

There are four major currency pairs that are used for trading more often than the rest. They are: US Dollar against Japanese Yen, US Dollar against Euro, US Dollar against British Pound and US Dollar against Swiss Franc. In the trading market they are represented as: USD/JPY, USD/EUR,

USD/GBP and USD/CHF. Another important thing to remember is that there are no dividends paid on currencies.

In the event that you feel that one of the currencies will appreciate against the other, you can switch between the two currencies of the pair. This way you can avoid suffering losses. When your predictions turn out to be true, you can switch back to the first currency. This way you can gain profits. You need to keep a track of the changing exchange rates in order to gain profits and/or avoid suffering massive losses in trading.

FOREX trading is an essential part of the worldwide market. Brokers at big banks perform FOREX transactions. The FOREX market is active throughout every working day. The dealers work in three different shifts every day in order to reduce the workload. This also decreases the chances of them committing mistakes.

Why is it important that the FOREX market is active 24/7?

The clients of the FOREX trading firms may place "take profit" or "stop loss" orders with the brokers. Read about what these orders are in case you aren't aware of them.

FOREX markets have an edge over stock markets in that the price movements on the FOREX market take place in a very smooth manner without any obstacles unlike those on the stock market. Another appreciable characteristic of the FOREX market is that the average daily turnover is around 1.2 trillion US dollars.

It is true that the FOREX market is active almost all the time. This market is the oldest and most widely used financial market of the world. Another name for the FOREX market is the foreign exchange market. It is also called the FX market for short. No other market works with a large amount of liquid money such as the foreign exchange market.

As mentioned before, no other financial market is anywhere nearly as big as the FOREX market. In comparison, even the currency futures market is a meager one percent as big as the foreign exchange market. The major difference between this market and the stock market is that trading does not involve exchanges. It is just the movement of funds between major banking firms of various countries such as the US, Australia, Japan, Great Britain, etc. Cash flows smoothly and the entire process does not encounter many obstacles.

The reason that small banking and trading firms could not participate in FOREX trading until recently is the large amounts required as minimum transactions and also the strict financial rules. These rules curbed the number of firms worldwide that could trade.

Due to recent technological advancements, the FOREX trading market is now open to smaller firms and has come a long way from where it started off. It is not as easy as it sounds and if you are new to the game, it is advisable to read as much as you can about it before actually participating.

Reasons to trade on the foreign exchange market

There are certain characteristics of the FOREX market that give it an edge over the other markets. These attributes provide an increased probability of gaining profits. The following are the advantages of trading on the foreign exchange market.

The market is open 24/7

An individual can take advantage of the market conditions at any point of time. You will not have to wait for the so-called opening bell that indicates the start of the day in the stock exchange market.

It uses liquid money

As mentioned earlier, the foreign exchange market is the most liquid financial market in the world. So whenever a trader wishes to exit the market, he or she can do so easily no matter what condition the market is in. There are minimal (almost non-existent) exit barriers and risks involved. Another advantage is that there is no daily trading limit.

High Leverage

The leverage ratio of the FOREX trading market is around 400. This increases the risk because if you suffer a loss, it will be massive. However, if you have a profitable transaction, the profits you gain are very large. This is an advantage and a disadvantage in itself.

The costs of the transactions are low

Under normal market conditions, retail transaction costs go as low as less than 0.1%. This is at normal firms. At larger firms, the required transaction cost could go even lower.

The FOREX market is always a bull market

A trade in the foreign exchange market is essentially the buying or selling of one currency against another. Therefore, whether the market is a bull market or a bear market is based on the value of a certain currency in other currencies. In case a certain currency has a higher value in another currency (for instance, the US dollar has a greater value than the Indian Rupee), the market can be a bull market if the trader purchases the currency against other currencies. On the flipside, if the currency has a lower value, a trader can gain profits by selling the currency against other currencies.

So, effectively, the FOREX market is always a bull market. The trader needs to know exactly what move to make when, in order to gain profits.

The Market between banks

The FOREX market is a global network. This network consists of people, called the dealers, who trade and communicate with their clients through telephones and the electronic network. In this market, there are no exchanges that have been organized.

The FOREX market is unregulated

There are certain banking laws that have to be adhered to by banks, which are the commercial dealers. Apart from that there is no authority that regulates the working of the FOREX Market. It has and always will be an unregulated market.

There are no laws that have been stated for the regular operations of the FOREX trading market. There are certain establishments all over the world dealing with the FOREX trading market. They have no reason to report their activities to the Revenue department in their Government!

What edge does FOREX have over futures or stock exchange?

As mentioned earlier, the foreign exchange market has a certain edge over the other two markets.

FOREX hàs a lower margin

As it is with futures and stock markets, a FOREX trader by putting up a small margin can gain the ability to control large amounts of money. The margins required for futures are generally around 5% of the effective value of the holding. In the stock exchange market, the margin is required to be around 50% of the total value of the stocks whereas in FOREX trading, the margin required is just 1% of the money invested. For instance, for trading every 1,000,000 dollars a margin of 10,000 dollars is required.

This effectively means that in FOREX trading, the trader can work with product whose value is around 5 times as much as the product of a futures trader and around 50 times as much as the value of the product of a stock broker.

When you are trading on the FOREX market, there is a very high probability of gaining profits. However, before you begin make sure you are familiar with the tactics needed and also make sure that you know the risks involved.

Another thing to make sure you fully understand is the working of your margin account. You must thoroughly read the margin agreement between you and your firm. The fact that it is important to know exactly how your margin account works cannot be overstated. For further queries, it is advisable to contact your account representative.

The trading firms set a predetermined amount of money below which the margin in your account must fall for the positions that you have in your account to be partially or completely liquidated. Chances are that you may not receive a margin call before your positions are liquidated.

No Commission and No Exchange Fees

When a person invests in futures trading, he or she needs to pay brokerage and exchange fees. One of the main advantages of FOREX trading is that it does not require any commission fee. This makes the entire process way easier. Foreign exchange trading is a worldwide market that directly matches the buyers with the sellers.

Although you do not have to pay the broker a commission fee for matching you with a buyer or seller (as the case may be), the spread is much larger than that involved in trading futures.

It is advisable to compare the commissions involved in both online FOREX trading and futures trading. The most expensive part of stock trading is the brokerage fees. So, most people prefer online trading.

Minimal risks and guaranteed stocks

As compared to futures trading and stock brokerage, foreign exchange trading has a much lesser risk involved. In fact, the risks involved in futures trading are very high. For instance, if you think that some company is going to increase its value over the next ten years or so, you will be tempted to invest a large chunk of money in them. You have enough proof to believe that they will be on the rise but then again, it is only a prediction and predictions can always go wrong. Of course, if the company does improve according to your prediction, your investment will pay off. On the flipside, if your prediction is wrong, you stand to lose a large amount of money. Furthermore, you will have to credit some money into your account in order to bridge the gap.

Rollover of Positions

It is only when your futures have expired that you have to wonder about whether or not you need to rollover your futures in order to stay in the trade. But when it comes to FOREX, you will have to rollover your trade every two days since the positions of your trade expires then! If you do not roll your trades over, you may not be able to stay in your position and may make a loss.

Chapter 2: How Does Forex Work?

To help you better understand the formula of buying and selling currencies, here are its two basic principles:

- When you buy a currency, you believe that such currency will get stronger, or increase in value, in a specific timeframe against the one you exchanged it for.

- When you sell a currency, you believe that such currency will weaken in a specific timeframe against the one you exchanged it for.

The price difference in buying and selling the currencies is where the profit or loss comes from.

To illustrate, let's take the EUR/USD for an example. After analyzing the price movement and reading about the latest economic news - which can significantly affect the price - you believe that the EUR will get stronger against the USD. So you BUY 15,000 Euros using US dollars with the current exchange rate of, let's say, 1.3608.

Buying: 15,000 euros = 20,412 USD

After a week, you SELL your Euros back to USD. By this time, the exchange rate is 1.4008.

Selling: 15,000 euros = 21,012 USD

In this scenario, you gained a profit of $600.00.

Reading the Forex Quote

As mentioned earlier, trading is always in pairs as we buy and sell currencies at the same time. The currency pair is divided with a "/" (or the slash) symbol.

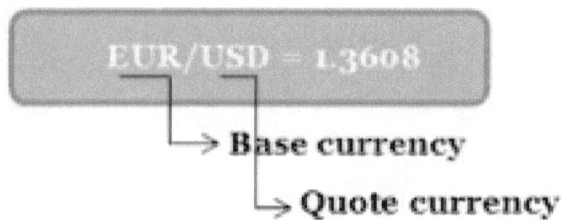

The currency on the left of the slash is the base currency; and the one on the right is the quote currency, also called the counter currency.

When buying, the quote currency will tell you how much you have to pay to have one unit of the base currency.

In the illustration earlier, to buy 1 Euro, you have to pay 1.3608 US dollars. On the other hand, when selling, the quote currency will tell you how much will you get from selling one unit of the base currency.

In the earlier example, for every Euro that you sell, you will have 1.3608 US dollars. Buying this pair means that you believe the EUR (base currency) will increase its value against the USD (quote currency), and selling this pair means you believe otherwise.

Essentially, the trade revolves around the base currency. When you hear the word buy or sell, it actually means buying or selling the base currency. In Forex, buying is also commonly termed as "taking the long position" or "going long" and selling is "taking the short position" or "going short."

The Bid and the Ask Price

Forex quotes are always quoted in two prices: the bid price and the ask price. The bid is the price a broker is willing to pay for your base currency when you sell them.

The ask price is the price of the base currency when you buy them.

Market Watch: 23:59:58

Symbol	Bid	Ask
◈ USDCHF	0.89814	0.89877
◈ GBPUSD	1.70828	1.70944
◈ EURUSD	1.35225	1.35262
◈ USDJPY	101.304	101.374
◈ USDCAD	1.07310	1.07352
◈ AUDUSD	0.93902	0.93983
◈ EURGBP	0.79137	0.79178
◈ EURAUD	1.43926	1.44050

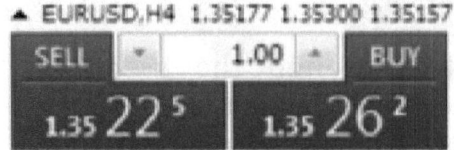

▲ EURUSD,H4 1.35177 1.35300 1.35157

SELL ▾	1.00 ▴	BUY
1.35 22^5		1.35 26^2

In the illustration above, a broker is willing to buy your Euros at 1.35225 USD, and they are selling it for 1.35262 USD at that same time. You will use the bid price if you are selling your base currency and you will use the asking price if you want to buy.

The difference between these two prices is called spread. This is where brokers and traders get their money. Although the spread is relatively small—in the example above, it is just 0.00037—when buying and selling in millions, it can easily make a good profit.

Pips and Pipettes

The movement of the price is measured in pips and pipettes. A pip is the last number, or the last decimal value, in a quote that has 2 and 4 decimal places. For example, when the EUR/USD's value moves from 1.3608 to 1.3607, which is 0.0001 USD price movement, you have one pip. However, there are currency pairs that quote in 3 or 5 decimal places. These fractional pips are called pipettes. If the GBP/USD moves from 1.71185 to 1.71186, then you have one pipette.

Lots and Leverage

In the past, Forex was traded in a standard size of 100,000 units. This means that traders should have at least 100,000 of the base currency if they want to sell or an equivalent in the quote currency if they want to buy. However, it changed when the internet began allowing the general public to participate in the market. Since most of the interested individuals don't have the required amount of money to start trading, brokers allow smaller lots and offer leverage.

The options of the lot size, or position, depend on the broker you signed up with and the type of account you have with them. There are brokers now that allow customized lot sizes.

Below are the most common lot sizes:

Lot	Number of Units
Standard	100,000
Mini	10,000
Micro	1,000
Nano	100

What if the required lot per trade with the broker signed up with is 10,000 units, and the trader only has 1,000 for his capital? Can he still trade?

The answer is yes. This is where leverage comes in.

Leverage allows traders to trade the minimum lot requirement by letting them borrow the remaining capital from their broker. This means that, even with a minimal deposit, the trader can have control over a large amount of money. This will help them maximize their potential profit.

However, brokers can't just cover the remaining cost to reach the minimum lot each time for any interested trader. They also have a condition called initial margin.

Initial margin, or account margin as it is also often called, is the required amount that the trader must cover per lot or position. This varies from broker to broker.

To illustrate this further, let's say you believe that the euro will go strong against the US dollars at the current exchange rate of 1.3607. You open a trade for one standard lot, which has 100,000 units; and the broker's account margin is 1 percent. This means that you are required $1,000(100,000 units x 1% margin) to open the trade.

After waiting and your predictions really did come true when the exchange rate reaches 1.3647, you then decide to sell. From this trade, the gain is $400.

Start of the trade

EUR/USD ask price	:	1.3607
Position	:	100,000
Leverage	:	100:1, or 1 percent
Margin	:	100,000 x 1% = $1,000

End of the trade

EUR/USD bid price	:	1.3647 (at the end of the trade)
Spread	:	1.3647 – 1.3607 = 0.004
Overall Profit	:	100,000 X 0.004 = $400

In this scenario, your deposit of $1,000 is then returned to you, and the profit will then be calculated by the system and credited to your account. As you can see, the profit of $400 from this example will not all go to your account as you leveraged during the trade.

Leverage is important as it allows the trader to earn a high profit with a minimal deposit and risk. There are brokers that offer leverage as high as 500:1, allowing an even smaller amount required to open the trade.

Chapter 3: Setting Yourself Up On the FOREX Market

Before you can get started on the FOREX trading market, there are a few things that you need to keep in mind. First and foremost, and most importantly, you will need to find and pick a broker you can trust to make your trades. In addition to the broker being good at what he does, you have to be able to trust him.

While choosing a broker to do your trading for you, you need to be aware of the fact that there are many types of FOREX brokers to pick from. The following are a few things you need to look for in a broker:

The broker should have low spreads

The spread of a currency pair is calculated in what is called pips. The spread is the difference between the price at which a currency can be bought and the price at which it can be sold at any point of time. The spread can keep varying. As FOREX brokers are not paid any commission, they make money through the spreads.

The difference in spreads between different FOREX traders is almost as large as the difference in commissions found in stock brokerage. This implies that you need a smaller spread in order to save your money. Therefore, it is better to hire a trader with a lower spread.

Extensive Tools and Research

Similar to the brokers in other markets, FOREX trading brokers offer various platforms through which trading can be done. Each platform shows various real-time charts and other statistical analysis. Before you commit to a broker, make sure to request free trials from the brokers. Brokers will also provide you with other research that will assist you. In short, you need to look for a broker who will provide you with everything you need to be successful in the market.

Account Types and leverage

Most brokers generally offer the client numerous account types to choose from. The smallest account and probably the safest for first-timers is called a mini account. These accounts require you to trade a minimum of around 300 US dollars.

This will provide you with a large amount of leverage. Leverage is something you will need in order to make profits with such a small amount of initial capital. Standard accounts allow you to work with a variety of leverages but these require a minimum initial capital of around 2000 US dollars.

Finally, there are accounts known as premium accounts. These accounts require a large amount of initial capital. One of the main advantages of these accounts is that they allow you to work with different amounts of leverage. In addition to that, they also provide you with other tools and services. The idea is to pick a broker who has the appropriate amount of leverage, tools, spread and services in accordance with the type of account you will be using for trading.

What is the Basic FOREX strategy?

You have learnt what the advantages of the FOREX are over futures and stocks. You have also been given a set pattern that you will have to follow when you choose to begin trading in the FOREX market. What is the next step? You will need to understand what strategy you will have to use in order to stay at the top of your game.

There are two strategies that most people use – Technical Analysis and Fundamental Analysis. These strategies are the same ones that are used in the stock market. However, for an individual trader it is best to use the technical analysis strategy. This chapter covers a basic review of these techniques and how they apply to FOREX trading.

Technical Analysis

The Technical Analysis in the stock market and the FOREX market deals with understanding and analyzing the trend line of the price of the stocks or trades respectively. The only difference between the usage of this strategy in the two markets is that for FOREX the analysis is conducted the entire day since the FOREX trading markets are open 24 hours a day!

It is due to this feature of the FOREX trading market that the different forms in the analysis that include the consideration of time have to be altered to fit the need of the FOREX trading market. There are millions of approaches that can be used to deal with this strategy. However, there are four methods that have been used most often.

1. The Fibonacci Studies

2. The Elliot Wave theory

3. Pivot points of the prices

4. The Parabolic SAR

There are a million technical analysts out there who will be ready to help you make accurate predictions of your trade of the FOREX trading market. They most often combine the first two methods that have been mentioned above to make the prediction. There are other analysts that create another virtual environment where they try to replicate the different conditions that affect the buying and selling of trades on the FOREX trading market.

Fundamental Analysis

It is hard to understand and analyze the value of company. It is harder to estimate the value of an entire country. This strategy is an extremely difficult one. This is often used to forecast the trend of the prices for a long period. There are certain traders that use this method to trade for short-term periods. But they do this based on the releases that have been made in the media, especially the news. There are multiple fundamental indicators that can be used to understand the currency values that have been released at different times during the day. There are certain indicators that you can keep tabs on in the beginning.

1. Consumer Price Index (CPI)

2. The Sale of retail products

3. Durable goods

4. Purchasing Manager Index (PMI)

You will have to understand that the reports for the aforementioned values are not the only things that you will need to have your eye on. You can attend different meetings that will help you understand and estimate the different quotes that you can make while trading and also see how these trades affect the market. These meetings are usually held to discuss any issue on the rates of interest, inflation, deflation and any other issue that made have the capacity of affecting the values of currency.

There are certain ways that the factors are worded in circulars or issues that may give every person a different perspective of the interest rates. This may cause a highly volatile market! You will have to make sure that you attend two meetings – the Humphrey Hawkins Hearing and the Federal Open market Committee. These meetings are of high importance.

As a fundamental analyst of FOREX, you will be able to gather a better insight if you read reports and also examine the different commentary that has been passed during the meetings. You will be able to understand the trends of the long market and also understand how you can profit through a short-term market. If you are using this strategy, you have to be sure that you have access to the reports and also maintain a calendar that will help you know when the report is coming out. You can hire a broker who will help you gather this information with ease.

How to choose your strategy

You will have to develop a strategy and learn how to perfect it in order to become a successful trader. There are people who focus only on a particular calculation or study. There are others that work on broadening their spectrum through an analysis in order to determine their trade. Certain experts state that you will need to try a combination of the aforementioned strategies in order to make a successful trading. They say that you will be able to determine when you can enter the marker and when you will need to exit the market. But it is you that has to decide what works best for your trade!

You will have to create a demo account that will help you understand the FOREX trading market with ease. You can practice using paper till you make consistent profit. There are beginners who tend to fail in the demo that they have been a part of and will directly jump into the actual FOREX trading market. They begin to lose all the money that they put in. You must take enough time to understand the games of the market, even if it means that you will need all the time in the world. Only when you are sure of the strategy and all the aspects of FOREX should you begin to work on money.

There is another important thing that you will have to learn. You will need to ensure that you keep a track of your emotions and ensure that you do not let emotions cloud your judgment when you have to trade. You will have to keep a track of your stop - loss points and make sure you execute them at the right times. If you do not execute these points strategically, you may make a loss. When you make a decision about your trades, stick to it!

You will realize soon enough that you have to follow the trend of the market. If you are going against the trend you are messing with the money that you have invested in the market. The FOREX market works on the trending prices. There is a high possibility that you will make a profit in the trading.

The FOREX market is one of the largest and most fascinating markets all over the world. There are people who have joined the market since they have become increasingly interested in the market. Before you begin the trading, zero in on the strategy that you would like to follow.

Chapter 4: When Is the Best Time To Trade?

Because Forex runs on a vast network of computers located in different time zones rather than in a single physical location, the market is open 24 hours. With this amount of time available, you might be wondering when is the best time to trade.

Before you can check which time you should be trading, it is important to know what happens in the market during a 24-hour period.

Figure 1. This Forex market hour graph is in EST. Source: Wave Power.

Let's explain the above picture. Sydney opens the Forex market every Sunday at 5PM. Two hours after Sydney opens, Tokyo's market also opens, creating a 7-hour overlap with Sydney's. Sydney and Tokyo markets close at 2AM and 4AM respectively.

Before Tokyo can close at 4AM, the London market wakes up and starts trading at 3AM; it ends at 12NN, overlapping with New York's market for 4 hours starting at 8AM. The market closes for the week at 4PM, when the New York market closes.

Now, let's explain what can happen when a nation's Forex market is in session.

A.   Tokyo Session

It's not surprising that the Japanese yen is the third most traded currency in the world as the country has a very strong export power. Twenty-one percent of all transactions that involve the Japanese yen happen during the Tokyo session as main market participants, like multinational companies and central banks, make their daily transactions. Most of the price movement can be seen in the early part of the session, when economic data is released and becomes available. Typically, at the later part of the day, there isn't much movement, unless there is a major announcement that affects the market.

What currency pairs should you trade?

At this time, it is best to trade according to the economic data or the current events from Australia, New Zealand, Japan, and China. Most of the time, there is higher movement in the AUD/JPY pair.

Take note that China's economic market is huge, and Australia and Japan has high import relations with this gigantic country. So whenever China releases economic news and forecasts, it can significantly create a price movement.

B.   London Session

The London session is the busiest time of the day, as thirty percent of all Forex transactions take place at this period. Because of the huge volume being traded at this time, transaction costs are potentially low. This session also usually offers the most volatility, allowing potential profit on any pair traded. However, this volatility typically dies down midway through the session as traders take their lunch breaks.

Although the trend during this session typically continues until the first few hours of the New York session, traders must watch out for price reversals at the end of the London session, It could happen when a significant number of traders decide to close their trade for the day - to either collect their profit or minimize their loss.

What currency pairs should you trade?

Although, as mentioned earlier, any pair can be traded at this time because of very high market activity across many major currencies, it is still recommended to stick to the major pairs, such as:

- EUR/USD

- GBP/USD

- USD/JPY

- USD/CHF

If you're looking for wider spreads, you can also trade euro and pound with Japanese yen.

C. New York Session

During the first few hours of this session, most trades are based on the trend during the London session—that is, if there wasn't any reversal. However, as a whopping 85 percent of the all Forex transaction involves the US dollar, economic news and reports released during the New York session can significantly pull up or drag down the price movements. Just like during the London session, almost any major currency pair can be traded at this time.

When to—and not to—Trade

Even if the market is open 24 hours a day, five days a week, it doesn't mean that you should be trading all these times on all sessions. Long-time Forex traders have determined that the trading time has a big role in their success - as it usually determines which currencies will give them the most potential profit.

It's Trading Time!

Here are the best trading times that bring in more profit:

Overlapping of two sessions. As two markets abuzz with activity, volatility - which translates to potential profitability - is high. This is especially true when the London and New York markets overlap.

Sessions	Overlaps
Sydney and Tokyo	7:00 pm to 2:00 am EST (EDT)
Tokyo and London	3:00 am to 4:00am EST
London and New York	8:00 am to 12:00 noon EST

1.   The London session

2.   The middle of the week.

The middle of the week - essentially Tuesday to Thursday - offers the most movement as more traders participate in the market. The spread typically widens at this time on almost all currency pairs.

Hold on to Your Money!

Here are the best times to hold on to your money as the market is either non-moving or too erratic:

1.   Sundays and Fridays.

This is the first five to six hours after Sydney opens the market on Sundays and the last four to five hours before New York closes on Fridays. These times have the least market activity as majority of the traders are still enjoying their weekend break.

2.   Holidays.

With no major market participants, like banks and multinational companies, and the majority of traders taking a break, movement is almost non-existent during these days - except when there is major economic news.

3.   Major news events.

This is when market prices drastically move up or down a significant notch, which could heap an equally significant profit—for an experienced and fast trader. However, for beginners, especially for those who have limited capital, the risk is too high that it is recommended to hold on to the money and wait.

4.   Major sports and entertainment competition events.

Traders also have their favorite team or rising stars. During these competitions, especially the finals, they could be cheering—or betting—for them, leaving the trader's chair vacant. Examples of these events are the Super Bowl, the NBA Finals, the World Series, and American Idol Finals Night.

PART II: Let's Start Investing & Trading!

Chapter 5: What Trader Type Are You?

On another note, if you feel you're enjoying the material so far, I'd appreciate it if you leave a positive review for the book! <u>Click here to leave a review.</u>

Anyways, moving on.

To become successful in this industry, you must determine what type of trader you will become. Although the system used is exactly the same, no two traders will have the same results. Your trading style highly depends on your personality and lifestyle. This is important as you might be forced to fit to a style that goes against your nature. When this happens, this can be stressful to you because you need to adjust and adapt each time - hindering you to reach your maximum potential in the long run.

There are four main different types of traders: scalpers, day traders, swing traders, and position traders.

A.   Scalpers

Scalpers are traders who enter the market numerous times a day. Their trade only last a couple of seconds to a few minutes. They prefer raking in small amounts of profits throughout the day than winning a one-time, big-time trade. Scalpers are people who:

-       like fast-paced, adrenaline-pumping work environments

-       have the ability to watch charts and graphs for hours and give it their undivided attention

-       are quick decision makers

-       have fast reflexes; they have to move fast when they trade because a few seconds have significant effects on the price

-       are impatient; can't stand waiting until the end of the day or for a few days to know if the trade has been won or otherwise

-       have very strong money management skills

-       have a very fast and reliable internet connection: prices reflected on the platform must be always real-time

Tips for Would-be Scalpers:

1.   It is recommended to trade currencies with the most liquidity, as you want to get the tightest spread. Remember: you will be entering the market numerous times a day.

2.   Trade when the market is abuzz with activity, which is highest when two markets overlap. It is recommended to do scalping during busiest overlaps, which is from 2:00 to 4:00 AM EST and 8:00 to 12:00 NN EST.

3.   Do not juggle multiple currency pairs, especially if you are a beginner. Focusing on one currency pair allows you to watch the charts and make quick, good trades when the opportunity presents itself. It also allows you to practice and hone your strategies with minimal risk.

Although there are traders who trade multiple currency pairs at a time, most of them have been scalping for a long time and have already developed their concentration. They can then make quick decisions - despite the large amount of information they need to process and consider.

4.   Watch out for possible economic reports and news. Always check the economic calendar for possible significant price changes in the next minute or hour. News reports have

the ability to throw scalpers' profits away - as it can cause price movements to abruptly change directions.

B.   Day Traders

Like scalping, day trading is also short-term. However, day traders only enter the market once and only once in a day. They put in their trade at the start of the day, monitor it throughout the day, and close it by the end of the day - no matter if they are winning or losing.

If the fast action in scalping is too much for you, but you also don't like holding on to your trade overnight, day trading is the best option to go.

This trading style fits people who:

-        want to know if they win or lose the trade by the end of the day

-        have the time to monitor their trade throughout the day

-        treat trading as their regular and full-time job

Tips for Would-Be Day Traders:

1.   Even if it possible to day trade while holding a full-time job at the same time, there is a disadvantage to it. Your attention will be divided between your job and the trade. You have to choose one, or else you have the potential to sacrifice both.

2.   Always, always keep yourself in the loop of all economic news and forecasts. This will significantly help you in your decision when making a trade at the start of the day.

C.   Swing Traders

Swing traders hold on to their trades for a couple of days. They analyze the market for a couple of hours each day, but they only enter the market when there's a medium-term trend —a trend that has been consistent in the last 24 hours or more —has been identified.

This technique allows the traders to enter the market only a very few times a week, mostly only once or twice, but traders have the benefit to maximize their profit and lower the risk by only entering the market when they have a higher probability of winning.

Swing trading is for people who:

-        want to make slower but surer trades

-        are patient in analyzing charts and economic data daily for a couple of hours to identify good trends

-        hold a full-time job but have a spare couple of hours to read charts and trade

-        don't easily panic

Tips for Would-be Swing Traders

1.   Since the trade is on for more than 24 hours, prices could go against the trader many times within the time frame of the trade. During these times, it is important not to panic. This is a normal occurrence in swing trades. Stay calm and trust in your analysis of the market.

2.   Have larger stop losses—the method in which the system will automatically close the trade when the price reaches a certain point (in the opposite direction) to minimize losses. This is to survive the volatility of the market. It is ideal to set it two or three times higher than the price range of the currency - on the day the trade is opened.

D.   Position Traders

Position trading is a long-term trading, lasting a couple of months to several years. Since the position is held on for a long time, traders must have a good grasp of the fundamental analyses (will be discussed in a later chapter) of the market, as well as the role it plays on the price movement.

Like in swing trading, the price movement could go against the trader multiple times during the duration of the trade. However, the movements are much bigger in position trading.

Position trading is the best option for people who:

-        has an in-depth understanding of how both national and international economic data can   affect a country's currency long-term

-        who don't mind waiting for a long time for a good profit, ranging from several hundreds to a few thousand pips

-        are not easily swayed by strong market opinions

-        have full trust of their analysis and have the skin to stick to it - despite the many significant things that could happen

-        have enough capital to withstand possible huge losses

Tips for Would-be Position Traders

Aside from being extremely patient and being able to stay calm, position traders must also have a strong understanding of the fundamentals. A position-style trader must be able to make an independent educated guess on where the market will go in a few months' or in a few years' time - based on the available economic reports and data.

Chapter 6: Technical Market Analysis

Now that you already have an idea on what trading style you will adopt, it is now time to get to know the three major types of market analyses. Learning how to succeed in the Forex market is a constant and never-ending process. There will always be something new to learn.

However, there are three basic analyses that serve as the foundation of all trading techniques. Though there are traders who argue that one is more important or helpful than the other, it is best to know all three as they have their individual functions.

Although, you can pick one, depending on your trading style, as your main guide. These market analyses will help you decide which position to take and maximize your chance of winning the trade.

The three basic types of market analyses are:

1.   Technical Analysis

2.   Fundamental Analysis

3.   Sentiment Analysis

Technical Analysis

Technical analysis is the strategy of looking into past price movements, both recent past and a couple of months or years past, to determine where the current price is headed. Since price reflects all economic data and activity, it is just right to study these prices as the same patterns and trends tend to repeat themselves. Additionally, since most traders use technical analysis, it also adds to the probability of having these price movements repeat themselves.

Technical analysis is heavy with graphs as they are the most effective way of laying out price movement in a specific period. It also helps spotting patterns easier.

There are three basic chart types:

A.   Line Chart

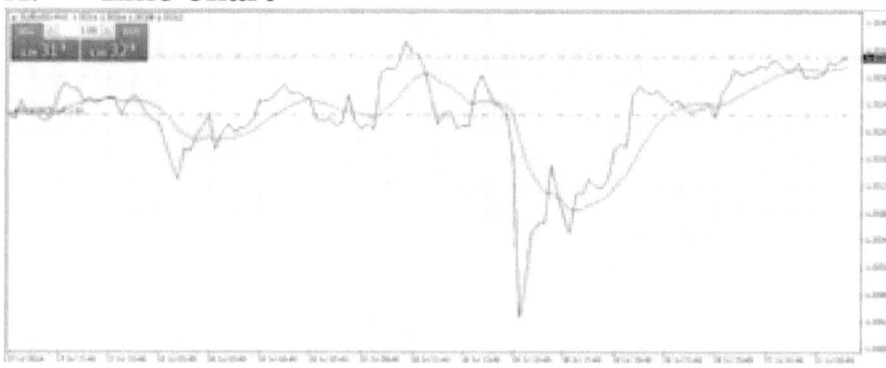

Here is what a line chart looks like. Line chart shows the closing price for each time period. For example, in the graph above, it shows the closing price of the EUR/USD every 15-minute interval.

B.   Bar Chart

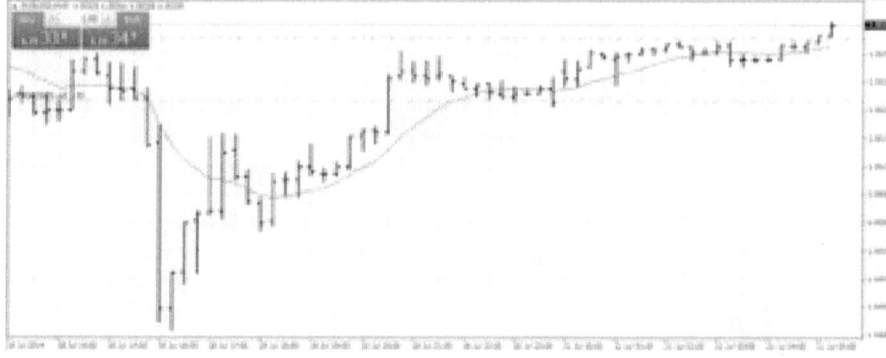

A bar chart is more detailed than a line chart. It shows the opening, closing, highest, and lowest prices in a time period.

Up close, this is how a bar looks like:

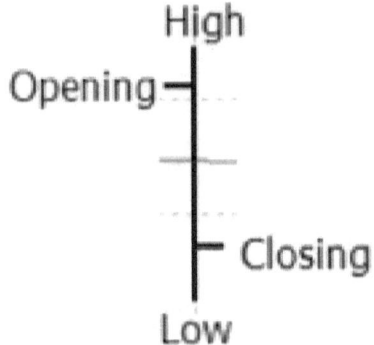

A bar could represent any segment of time, depending on what interval the trader set it. It could represent an hour, a 4-hour interval, a day, a week, or a month. So, when somebody referenced you to a bar, make sure to know what time frame it represents.

Here are the parts of a bar:

-       Opening–

The horizontal line on the left side of the vertical line is the opening price of a time period.

-       High –

The highest point of the vertical line is the highest price the currency has reached that specific time period.

-       Low–

The bottom of the vertical line is the lowest price the currency has reached for that specific time period.

-        Closing –

This is the point where the price is at the end of a time period.

C.   Candlestick Chart

Candlestick is the most commonly used chart because it provides a more effective visual representation of the market. It gives the trader the information from a bar chart, plus whether the market closes higher or lower than the opening price. This is how a candlestick chart looks like:

Typically, traders use green if the price at the end of a time period is higher than the opening price, and red if otherwise.

However, the classic candlestick bar is blocked and hollow, like this:

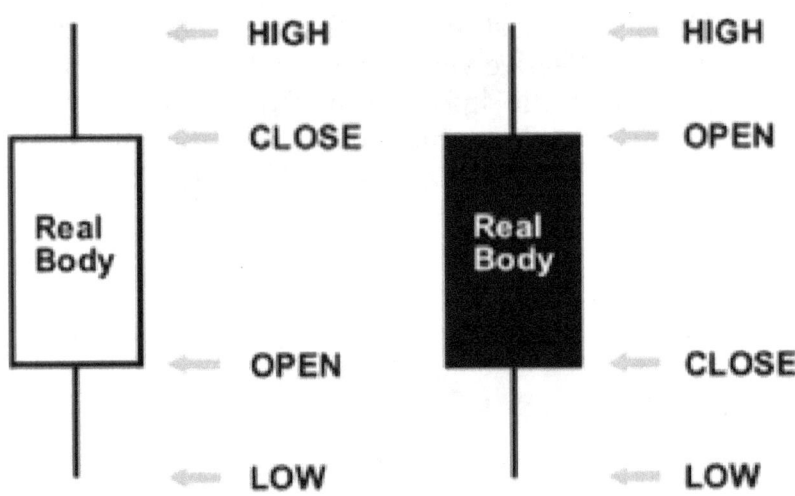

If the market closes higher than the opening price, it is represented with a hollow or unfilled body. Otherwise, it's a filled one if it closed below the opening price.

If these typical colors do not suit your preference, you usually have the option to customize the colors of your charts.

Chapter 7: Fundamental and Sentiment Analyses

Fundamental Analysis

Fundamental analysis is a trading technique of looking into the overall economic performance of a country, which could indicate the strength of its currency. The main principle of fundamental analysis revolves around the basic idea of economics: supply and demand.

If a country has good social, political, and business data, fundamental analysts take it as an indicator that there is - or there will be - a high demand of the country's currency. This makes its prices surge upward, as investors and speculators make transactions with the country or with the people from that country.

This is where factors, such as unemployment, political unrest, real estate conditions, natural calamities, and change in monetary policies are digested and used as an instrument to predict where the price might head in future. Basically, with fundamental analysis, a good economy translates to a higher currency value and a bad or shaky economy is to lower currency value.

Unlike technical trading, where there are specifics in the price movement, fundamental analysis has too much data available for a trader to consider. This is added with the fact that the trader has to look at reports of both countries of the currency pair he/she considers trading.

However, the fundamentals are equally important because a major news report can easily topple the patterns and trends that technical analysts are suggesting. On the other hand, technical analysis can also present short-term trading opportunities that might be too blurry with the fundamentals.

Here are the factors that might affect the fundamental analysis:

1. interest rates

2. monetary policy

3. change of leadership within central banks

4. long-term market movers

5. news, market data, financial reports

6. market reaction

Sentiment Analysis

Even if two traders are looking at the same data on a price chart, heard or read the same economic news, and are looking to trade the same currency pair, they will not always have the same "feel" about the market. Basically, each trader reacts differently to the same market conditions. The dominating feeling or idea of all market participants is called the market sentiment.

While the charts in technical trading will give you specifics on where you should enter and exit the market, sentiment-based trading will tell you whether you should be trading with the majority or going against them. You have the freedom to gauge the overall market reaction, anticipate price movement based on the said reaction, and make a trade based on this assessment.

For example, troubling European economic news has just been released. You think that this news will have most traders sell their euros in no time to minimize loss. After the panic selling, when the price really did drop drastically, you go against the market and buy euros because you believe that the euros will soon recover. This is an example of sentiment trading. You react based on the current or anticipated market emotion.

Chapter 8: Choosing the Right Broker

Now that you have learned what Forex is and how can you turn it into a financial opportunity, it is time to select your broker for you to get started. You might have read about brokers saying their traders make a couple of hundred to a few thousand dollars in a day - or in a couple of minutes.

The pop-up online advertisements and on TV—and yes, they sound tempting—but you should always be wary of these claims. While such huge profit can be possible in a short timeframe, a lot of scheming individuals and companies take advantage of the confusion and too-many unknowns of the general public.

They use this type of exaggerated claims to lure people to invest their hard-earned money on them, without telling them the real risk of trading. Instead, they even advertise guaranteed profits, which simply do not exist in this type of moneymaking opportunity.

Below is guide on how to choose the right broker for you and avoid the many scams out there:

Criteria No. 1: Regulation, Country the Broker is based from, and Reputation

The most important thing that you must consider when choosing a broker is to check if they are regulated or registered by the Commodity Future Trading Commission (CFTC) or National Futures Association (NFA) if they are based in the US; by the Financial Service Authority (FSA) if they are based in the United Kingdom; and by an equal authority from where the broker is based.

However, checking their registration is not enough. Signing up with a broker from a country that has strong legal protection will also help minimize the risk. Avoid brokers from countries who are currently experiencing strong political upheavals and are engaged in wars. This usually makes recovering lost money impossible whenever disputes arise.

Additionally, reputation must also be considered. Check the traders' reviews on the broker and also check what complaints have been filed against the company. Check if these complaints have been addressed by the company, as well.

Criteria No. 2: Capitalization

Capitalization plays an equally important role in making sure that your capital will not be lost in limbo.

A few years back, CFTC found out that there are brokers who had less than $100,000 for their capital. There is high risk when a broker is undercapitalized; they may not be able to cover even the operational costs. Also, the traders are exposed to a very high chance of not being able to withdraw their profits, or even their capital, whenever they want to.

Because of this, CFTC implements the rule that set the minimum capital at $20 million for all Forex brokers. Regulating bodies in other countries followed suit. For information whether the broker you're planning to sign up is well capitalized, you can check the official website of the regulatory body. They are usually updated monthly.

Criteria No. 3: Trading Platform

MetaTrader is one of the standard trading platforms out there. Although MetaTrader 5 is already available, offering more advanced features, majority of the brokers still use MetaTrader 4. Even now, it is still the number one preference among traders as they are already familiar with the usual features that come with it. Features include using trading robots, as well as importing market indicators and graphs from various sources on the internet. However, there are also other trading platforms, such as ACT Forex and Dealbook 360 from GMT among others. These platforms can also offer the same features as MetaTrader 4.

Even if choosing a platform boils down to personal preference, the best way to pick it is through demo trading. You will be spending most of your time on the platform so it is important to make sure that you are really comfortable of its interface and functionalities.

And always, always take advantage of the demo trading offered by your potential brokers, as it will give you a feel of the live trading. If the broker does not offer any demo accounts on their platforms, seriously consider picking a different broker.

Criteria No. 4: Broker Type, Spreads, and Commissions

As a trader, you must know that there are two kinds of brokers: the dealing desk broker, which also called the market maker and the non-dealing desk broker.

1.   Dealing Desk Brokers or Market Makers

Dealing desk brokers earn their money from the difference between the asking prices and bid prices they quote for a currency pair - in other words, the spread. They have the discretion on how much to quote for the bid and ask price since they do not actually see the real prices from the interbank market. However, the tight competition among dealing desk brokers allows the prices to be same or very close to the actual market prices.

Dealing desk brokers are also called market makers because they literally make a market for the traders. For example, when a trader places a buy order with them, they find someone among its clients who will take the opposite trade.

This way, their loss is minimized, as they don't have to place an opposite trade.

However, most of them have a liquidity provider, a private individual or a company who readily buys and sells. In case these two options are not available, then the dealing desk broker has to place the opposite trade himself.

2.   Non-dealing Desk Brokers

Non-dealing desk brokers do not take the opposite side of their clients' trade. Instead, they let all participants—which could be retail traders, brokers themselves, banks, and hedge funds—trade against each other, making the best bid and ask price. Therefore, expect the prices to be very tight. Non-dealing desk brokers, also called ECN (electronic communication network) brokers, earn through a small commission per trade.

Criteria No. 4: Ease of Depositing and Withdrawing Funds from Your Account

One of the top complaints of traders about their brokers is the tedious and slow process of withdrawing the profits they gained. There is no reason why your broker should hold on to the money you rightfully own, so withdrawals should be fast and easy. Make sure that the broker you're signed up with has good reputation on this area.

Criteria No. 5: Availability of Customer Service

There will always be something that we won't easily get by ourselves or something that we need to clarify. In Forex trading, it is best to ask questions on anything that you are not sure or confused about. Make sure that your broker's customer support or live agent is easily available. Most of the time, the customer support staff also doubles as your account manager. They have the goal of keeping you in the business. Usually, the first person who assisted you will be the person who will assist you all the way. However, there are still brokers who have major issues with their customer support. Stay away from them.

What Type of Broker Should You Sign Up With?

One type of broker is not necessarily better than the other. It really depends on your trading style. If you prefer short time trading, entering the market once or a couple of times a day, then you might benefit from the tighter spread. However, you must take note that you will be paying a commission per trade.

On the other hand, if you are a swing or a position trader, the wider spreads may be of less significance. It all boils down to tighter spread with commissions to be paid against wider spreads minus the commission.

PRACTICE: Trading Platforms

Here's the link to the MetaTrader website: www.metatrader.com

Feel free to download the software if you like. Use it to get a handle on Forex trading, as well as to see everything you've learned so far - live in action. Feel free to also explore the site if you have any further questions about MetaTrader.

The software is available for iOS, Android and Windows mobile devices. It's also available on Windows and Mac.

Chapter 9: But First, Your Demo Account

With the necessary details on how the Forex market operates, it is now time to put your skills to test. However, this does not mean that you need to jump right in and do your first trade, risking your hard-earned money big time!

Even if you can already start trading after reading this book, honing your skills and polishing your trading strategy are the goals to increase your chances of winning the trades and staying in the game. To do this, always start with demo trading.

Demo Trading

With demo trading, you get to feel how the real scenario works because you will be looking at real data but trading with virtual money. With this, you get to test your strategies and see which works best, without risking of losing your capital.

Until when should you be doing demo trading?

How would you know that you are ready for the live market? Forex experts recommend to do demo trading for at least three to six months. However, you have the freedom not to stick to this recommendation if we factor in the number of hours you spend doing it.

You could start trading sooner or later than this suggested time frame, but it is important that when you do, you already have more winning than losing trades, that there is a positive balance and a good profit in the demo account after countless trades, and that you are already confident with your trading strategy.

Opening a demo account almost has the same process as opening a live one; the only difference is there is real money involved in the latter.

PRACTICE: Your Demo Account

Here are some of the most notable Demo Forex Trading accounts around.

You know what to do with them.

- AvaTrade
- FxPro. com
- GCI Trading

Have fun!

Chapter 10: A Guide to Opening a Forex Account

If you feel confident with Forex, after a long string of consistent and successful runs with your demo account, it may be time to start opening a REAL Forex trading account.

Below are the steps on how to open a Forex trading account, given that you have already chosen a broker:

1.   Choose an account type.

There are two basic types of Forex accounts: a personal account and a business account.

Choose a personal account if you want to continue with your goal of becoming a trader and you want to put your months of practice to test.

However, if you think other people can grow the money for you, then open a business account. This usually requires a minimum of $25,000 deposit.

Business accounts are managed accounts. You will be assigned an account manager who will do the trades for you. For every winning trade, he/she gets a cut of the profit.

2.   Register.

To open an account, you have to go to the broker's website and choose to open either a live or a demo account. You need to fill out the basic personal and financial information, just like the demo accounts from before.

There are also some brokers that ask you to download the forms in PDF format and have them filled out. If you have questions or concerns about the registration process, nine out of ten brokers have available live chat agents or customer support ready to assist you anytime. After the information has been submitted, your broker might need additional documents from you to confirm your identity or address. You might be asked to upload a scanned copy of your ID and a proof of address.

Additionally, take note that wiring out your money to your broker for your deposit may cost more than you think. Check with your bank first before you make the transaction as the fees may cut a significant portion of your capital.

3.   Account activation.

After all required documents have been submitted and information has been verified, you will typically receive e-mail from your broker on how to proceed with the process.

After the deposit has been confirmed, you will also receive another e-mail stating such.

After your account has been activated, you should receive a final e-mail that contains your login information. From the broker's website or from an e-mail link, you can download the platform that they are using (usually MetaTrader 4), put in your username and password once it's already up and running, open the charts, and start trading. It is that easy.

However, again, it is strongly recommended to do demo trading first!

Whenever you have questions about the process, trade, and the costs, do not ever hesitate to seek out and ask experts.

PART III: Stay in the Game!

Chapter 11: Tips on Succeeding In Forex

Anyone can gain huge profit in a short period of time in Forex trading, but it is also not a secret that anyone can lose all his or her capital in the first day.

That's why we can't emphasize enough the importance of demo trading before going live. As mentioned earlier, learning about Forex trading is a constant and never-ending process as you develop your own trading plans and strategies; however, long-time Forex traders who have proven themselves have agreed on certain rules that help them stay in the game.

Here are the top trading tips that every trader should know:

1.   Start gradually.

Even if you have been demo trading for quite some time, the emotions that the live market brings is more compelling. So it is better to get used to the real rush and blow without risking losing all of your money at the soonest possible time. There are different recommended amounts to trade when you are starting; however, this is dependent on how much you have in your account. By this, we recommend you risk at most 1/6 of your balance on each trade.

2.   Use multiple time frames.

A one-day interval chart or shorter will give you exact locations of your entry and exit points in the market, but this does not mean that you have to ignore the weekly or monthly charts as they are also effective in spotting trends.

3.   Know when to close and when to continue to trade.

Although this is one of the most common mantra professional Forex brokers have been giving out, this is the hardest to practice. Because what usually happens is that when traders see that the market is doing well, and they are earning, they tend to close the trade very soon - out of fear the market might change directions.

On the other hand, when the market goes the opposite direction and their profits starts to register the negative sign, traders tend to "wait" in the hopes that the price movement will change anytime soon - only to be pushed deeper, resulting in big losses.

If the market looks promising, allow the trade to continue. If you are losing, it is better to close early.

4.   If the market is too erratic to predict and you can't afford to miss one trade, follow the experts.

Forex experts are there for a reason. They have honed their skills to stay afloat no matter where the market goes. But, of course, they don't have winning trades all the time.

However, if the market is too jumpy for you because of certain data recently released, follow the experts' lead. Trading platforms now usually have a feature that allows you to follow traders who have more profitable trades on an average and see what position they take.

5.   Develop your own trading strategy.

This takes some time to do and more patience—and maybe more demo trading—but the effort will be worth it as you develop a deeper understanding of the market. When you are putting your strategies to test, especially if you are doing long-term trading, even if the market is going against you, trust in your strategy and stick to it. You will have enough time to tweak it once you determine which factor did not work.

6.   Never stop learning.

Connect and engage with fellow Forex traders on forums and communities, especially those who have been trading for a long time. Learn from them. Consistently read more articles, blogs, and books on the topic.

There are a few other tips that you can always use to your advantage while trading on the FOREX. This section covers a few more tips!

1. If you know that a position is losing, do not add your money to it. This is common sense. There are chances that you may make a mistake on account of being a beginner.

2. You must only exit the trade if you understand the changing circumstances. It is pointless to exit a trade if you find yourself making a profit.

3. You will have to identify the times when you do not have to trade at all. There are different external factors like liquidity that you will need to consider.

4. You will need to learn the power that you gain if you own a position. Remember to never make any trades on the market if you have your own position.

5. There are certain strategies that you follow that may work in either the up market or the down market. The strategy for one will not work for the other. It is always good to acknowledge this fact.

6. You will find it very easy to enter a losing trade,

7. Buy all the news you can get about FOREX.

8. You should always go with your gut. If you feel that you should not get into a trade, do not do it!

9. The first and the last trade are always the most expensive. You will need to ensure that you get in late but that you get out early!

Chapter 12: Your Mindset, and The Role It Plays

The Forex market is a very emotional market.

Emotion is a powerful element that has the ability of making a trader drop their trading plan in an instant or sway from their strategy.

You must be prepared for it by having a good mindset. A good mindset is what pulls all the practical knowledge you have gained together and stay focused on your goal.

Below are important points to remember before entering and when already in the market:

1.   Be realistic about your expectations.

Let go of the idea that you can quit your regular job and have Forex trading as your main source of income - in a month. Do not focus on the results. Focus on the process and it will take care of the result. Learn as much as you can. Understand how much you have in the account and how much risk you can handle per trade. Additionally, only trade with "unimportant" money—that is, money you are okay to lose, because you really COULD lose it all.

2.   Have quality trades.

There is no good in entering the market a couple of times each day when you are losing money faster than you earn. Slow down and only trade when you are confident of the trend or the outcome of the market. Do not just guess. Do not gamble.

3.   This is not a get-rich quick scheme.

Yes, Forex trading can be a very profitable income opportunity, but you have to understand the risks and be willing to learn the ropes to be successful. It DOES take time, effort, and - more importantly - practice. But that's not just Forex Trading; it's EVERY major business or investing/ trading campaign out there.

Conclusion

Thank you again for downloading this book!

I hope this book was able to help you.

The next step is to apply what you've learned.

Finally, if you enjoyed this book, please take the time to share your thoughts and post a review on Amazon. It'd be greatly appreciated!

If you truly received value from this book, then I'd like to ask you a favor.

Would you be kind and courteous enough to leave a good review on Amazon?

I aim to reach as many like-minded people as I can with this book. More reviews will help me accomplish that!
Also, if you happen to be a writer or any type of artist as well, you may even have some good karma; your   odds of having more great reviews for your books increases :)

P.S. Things change. Trends change. And so will this book. As a token of appreciation for your commitment to downloading this book, enjoy all the free updates to this book version in the future. Take care.

BONUS: Successful Real Estate Investing

Courtesy of FR Commerce, enjoy a few free chapters of our other books.

If you want to learn more, please visit the Book Page.

"Intro"

" With the concept of real estate, the first thing that comes to people's minds is selling and buying houses.

Some think that you need to have excellent communication and marketing skills in order to succeed in your career if you're into real estate. They say that it's all about the talk, the eye contact, and the perfect sales pitches to say. But then again, there's more to real estate than selling houses and good sales talk.

Real estate is very a stable business to be part of. One of the basic needs in life is shelter; a habitat that can keep you safe and protected from whatever dangers and weather out there. A house is more than a structure. It's a place to call home; a sanctuary.

On the business of real estate, it is actually land and anything that is attached to it - with value. It deals with anything and everything that has to do with property and land ownership. And always remember: location is everything. It really is all about the location.

In terms of money, real estate can be very lucrative. Learn all the terminology and the basic fundamentals, and not only will you be able to survive long enough to know the ropes - you'll thrive. Along the way, familiarize yourself with a list of common real estate terms and their meanings. By then, you are ready for the actual business of real estate.

As beginners, it is important to know the fundamentals of real estate before going out into the field. There's a lot more to the business of real estate than just putting up vacant properties and houses for sale or rent. There are investment policies and mortgages to learn, and common mistakes you need to avoid. On top of that, you may have to exercise your communication skills to understand and communicate better with other people – clients, investors, and customers. "

View SUCCESSFUL REAL ESTATE INVESTING, by F.R. Commerce, exclusively on Amazon TODAY!

"Rental Income"

"Making money from renting out property is a very lucrative source of income.

A great illustration of that would be a game of monopoly. If you have interest in a house, an apartment building, a hotel or an office building, then you can rent those out and collect rent in exchange for letting them utilize those buildings.

A useful tool in making money from these properties is the capitalization rate. This rate is a special financial ratio: the value for the property on sale is divided by the value they earn per year. For instance, your apartment building may be sold for a million dollars, yet it earns one hundred thousand dollars a year in rental income. One million dollars is divided by the hundred thousand dollars - which gives us a ratio of 10 percent. Thus, you can expect a 10 percent return on your investment if you purchased the said property in cash and without any debt in acquiring it.

If you still want to use debt to acquire that property, it's still quite advantageous. As long as the rental income exceeds the monthly mortgage or loan cost, cash and equity still goes into your pocket.

"Business Operations"

This type of operation involves business activities and special services. For instance, you are the owner of an office building and you may generate income through vending machines placed in the building and for pay parking. You are able to earn income not just by renting your property out, but by providing income-generating goods and services. In addition, you can also rent out your property, or have a business that you operate."

View SUCCESSFUL REAL ESTATE INVESTING, by F.R. Commerce, exclusively on Amazon TODAY!

BONUS: Successful Stock Investing

Courtesy of FR Commerce, enjoy a few free chapters of our other books.

If you want to learn more, please visit the Book Page.

"Preview"

" *The realm of the affluent are well too familiar with the world of stocks. They know where and how to invest their amassed fortunes, only to grow those fortunes even further as their investments grow in value. Also, those same investments continue to pay off the owners somehow - through dividends, interest, gains, and so on.*

But here's the best news. That skill - successfully investing in stocks - is not limited to just the affluent. Fortunately, you don't need to have a business degree to earn profits in stocks either.

But first...

Are you willing to learn further?

Are you not afraid to fail?

Do you have the will and focus to move forward? No matter how bad the news and markets blare at you?

If you answered yes to all the above, carry on. (if not, you may wanna return this book. Stocks are NOT for the weak!)

Good. now let's move forward.

The following first few chapters introduce you to the world of stocks. They will give you some background in stocks, so you'll be able to understand how this investment product works and how it can help you build your wealth.

In the next chapters, by practicing some simple guidelines such as making regular investments in proven companies, risks can be minimized. Adequate knowledge can help you make sound decisions. Hence, the most basic rule in investing is: Know what you're getting into! "

View SUCCESSFUL STOCK INVESTING, by F.R. Commerce on Amazon TODAY!

" Defining the Stock Market "

Market Types Explained

Perhaps you have heard about primary markets and secondary markets and you might have wondered what its relevance to the stock market is. You may have even asked yourself how many stock market types are there...

Primary Markets

On the one hand, securities are created (via IPO – Initial Public Offering) in primary markets. It is basically a market in which companies sell stocks to the public for the first time.

When a company decides to go public, a set of requirements has to be fulfilled first.

One, an underwriting firm should be contacted to identify the legal and financial details of a public offering.

Two, filing of a preliminary registration statement, known as the preliminary prospectus, should be made with the appointed authorities. The statement should detail the company's prospects and interests. Note that this document is neither a solicitation nor is it finalized. It is simply a set of documents that describes the company's intent.

Three, the appointed authorities must approve the finalized statement and the final prospectus, the document that details the stock price, benefits, restrictions. It is a legally binding document for the company and its would-be shareholders. In primary markets, the stocks are purchased straight from the issuing company.

Secondary Markets

When people talk about the stock market, they usually refer to the secondary market. It is formally defined as the venue where investors can trade previously issued securities minus the involvement of the issuing companies.

In the secondary market, investors buy shares from other investors. This is what we commonly recognize as the "stock market". It encompasses the New York Stock Exchange, Nasdaq, and all the other exchanges around the globe. In this case, the issuing company is not involved in any way in the exchange. Investors trade with fellow investors who own the shares that you would like to either buy or sell.

Secondary markets are further subdivided into auction markets and dealer markets:

Auction Market

A feature of an auction market is that all parties interested to trade securities, either as an individual or institution, assemble in an area and announce their target buying or selling price - or the bid and ask price. The aim of this system is to bring all parties together until each has found a counterpart offering an agreeable deal.

Dealer Market

In the case of a dealer market, all parties do not have to assemble in a central hub. Market participants are connected via electronic networks. In this system, the dealers have an inventory of securities which they can buy or sell to the market participants. Different dealers offer a spread of prices where they would like to buy or sell the securities. This option gives investors an idea of the best possible price that they can avail in making a trade.

View SUCCESSFUL STOCK INVESTING, by F.R. Commerce on Amazon TODAY!

BONUS: Successful Options Trading

Courtesy of FR Commerce, enjoy a few free chapters of our other books.

If you want to learn more, please visit the Book Page.

"A lot of people are afraid to try options trading. They feel that it is so complex that only scientists can understand it.

But, there's no need to be so hesitant.

Because the basics of option trading are easy to understand - there's a good learning experience here that helps those who need the guidance.

First, you may not realize it, but you can essentially control the underlying assets - the stock, bond, or other commodity within the option contract - within the given time frame. You have the "option" (no pun intended) to buy, sell, hand over the rights, or just hold on to them. Did the stock price suddenly skyrocket? Imagine buying that same stock for a really low price. Did the stock price suddenly drop? Imagine selling that same stock at the original price. Your choices are virtually endless.

Next, Some investors prefer buying options instead of the underlying asset because the former is cheaper to buy than the latter. Furthermore, they can control the number of shares for a lesser price.

The first two parts introduce you to the world of options. They differentiate between stocks themselves and the options bound to them. They also show you how options work and all the terms options use.

The next parts will send you into the fire: you will be armed with various strategies, as well as do's and don'ts as you start your options campaign.

If you feel more than confident enough to take on the real world of options, try your hand on the real money online exchanges - and trade your way into victory. "

View OPTIONS TRADING SUCCESSFULLY, by F.R. Commerce today!

Options and Leveraging, for example:

Let's say an investor purchased 100 shares of a particular company stock at $100 each. Therefore, it has cost him $10,000. However, he also has five $200 premium call options each with a $100/share strike price, which will allow him the right to purchase 500 shares as well.

If after 1 month the share price rose to $110, the gain on his stocks is $1,000. However, what if the option premium for the same stock also increases - to $300 for each whole contract?. For the regular stock investment, the gain is 10%; for his stock option values, the gain is 50%.

But for ALL the underlying stocks within his five options, he can exercise all the options, buying 500 more originally at $50,00 overall, then SELLING them back at $55,000 - that's a $5,000 profit.

Leveraging has its disadvantages, too. If the price didn't move to the right direction, the percentage lost is magnified.

Using the same example, if the share price fell to $80 ($10 lower than the option's strike price), the loss is 20%. On the other hand, the option premium might decrease to $80, or a 60% percentage loss overall.

As such, an investor must exercise caution in using leveraging when trading options.

Time Frame

A regular stock has no expiration date. It means that the stockholder can hold onto his stocks indefinitely. On the other hand, a stock option has an expiration date. An out-of-the-money option only becomes worthless when it is not exercised prior to its expiration date.

Ownership

Ownership of a share of stock is proven by a certificate issued by the company. A stock option doesn't have a certificate of ownership; whoever holds it owns it.

Volume

A company can only issue a fixed number of shares. Therefore, investors can only trade a limited number of shares. On the other hand, there us no limit as to the number of stock options investors can buy or sell. A stock option doesn't offer dividends, voting rights, or ownership of the company if the option isn't exercised.

Market Exchanges

Professional traders, individual investors, and institutions trade options on an options exchange. It is possible for an entity to transact a lot of options contracts at the same time.

Like regular stocks, a stock option is traded on a market regulated by SEC. Brokers facilitate the options transactions just like the regular stocks. Monitoring of transactions and performances are easily done through their respective marketplaces.

View OPTIONS TRADING SUCCESSFULLY, by F.R. Commerce today!

www.ingramcontent.com/pod-product-compliance
Lightning Source LLC
Chambersburg PA
CBHW021412170526
45164CB00002B/615